CHINA

By Charis Mather

All rights reserved.
Printed in Poland.

A catalogue record for this book is available from the British Library.

ISBN: 978-1-80155-588-3

Written by:
Charis Mather

Edited by:
William Anthony

Designed by:
Drue Rintoul

©2022
BookLife Publishing Ltd.
King's Lynn, Norfolk
PE30 4LS, UK

All facts, statistics, web addresses and URLs in this book were verified as valid and accurate at time of writing. No responsibility for any changes to external websites or references can be accepted by either the author or publisher.

Image Credits

All images are courtesy of Shutterstock.com, unless otherwise specified. With thanks to Getty Images, Thinkstock Photo and iStockphoto.

Cover – IHOR SULYATYTSKYY, sleepingpanda. 2-3 – aphotostory. 4-5 – Fabio Nodari, Alex Staroseltsev. 6-7 – T. Lesia, HelloRF Zcool. 8-9 – linlypu, sevenke. 10-11 – Anna Polukhina, crazybike, Dragon Images, Peiling Lee, SeventyFour. 12-13 – Liudmila Kotvitckaia, Aquarius Studio, Romix Image, norikko, nantarpats. 14-15 – Martinez de la Varga, flysnowfly. 16-17 – gyn9037, Xiangli Li. 18-19 – Tatiana Popova, DnDavis. 20-21 – miszaszym, Jono Photography. 22-23 – Yuri Yavnik, Lukasz Kurbiel.

CONTENTS

Page 4   Country to Country
Page 6   Today's Trip Is to... China!
Page 8   Beijing
Page 10   Chinese New Year
Page 12   Food
Page 14   Panda Bears
Page 16   China's Rivers
Page 18   Terracotta Army
Page 20   Amazing Buildings
Page 22   Before You Go...
Page 24   Glossary and Index

Words that look like <u>this</u> can be found in the glossary on page 24.

COUNTRY TO COUNTRY

What country do you live in?

Countries are areas of land and the people that live there. People in different countries usually have their own ways of living and their own rules. Countries usually have clear **borders** that are drawn on maps.

There are many countries in the world that have their own interesting things to see and do. What country do you think we are going to visit in this book?

How many countries have you been to?

TODAY'S TRIP IS TO...
CHINA!

China is a country in the continent of Asia. A continent is a large area of land that is usually made up of lots of countries. Can you see where China is on the map?

FACT FILE

Capital city: Beijing
Main language: Mandarin Chinese
Currency: Renminbi
Flag:

Currency is the type of money that is used by a country.

BEIJING

We are in Beijing. Beijing is the capital city of China. It has many large, **modern** buildings made of glass and metal. If you go to Beijing, you might see some of these famous sights.

Beijing's modern buildings are home to millions of people.

Beijing is also known for its long history. Historical buildings called siheyuan are quite different from Beijing's modern buildings. They have four sides around an open area. There are still some siheyuan in Beijing today.

CHINESE NEW YEAR

Chinese New Year is China's biggest **celebration**. Families get ready by cleaning their houses and decorating. Many people go out to watch the fireworks. Some places have amazing dragon dances.

People travel a long way to be with their families.

Most families celebrate by meeting together for a big meal. There are lots of dishes, including dumplings, sticky rice cake and fish. Older family members give children red envelopes full of money as gifts.

Red is a lucky colour in China.

FOOD

Different parts of China have different types of food. Some Chinese people eat noodle dishes as their main food, and some eat rice dishes. Chinese food can be salty, sweet, spicy, sour or a mix.

Most Chinese dishes are eaten with chopsticks.

Here are some popular Chinese foods:

Dumplings
These are filled with meat and vegetables.

Noodles
Some people have noodles for breakfast.

Hotpot
This meal is to share. Everyone adds and cooks their favourite food in the soup.

PANDA BEARS

Panda bears are China's most loved animal. Some pandas live in mountain forests where they can find lots of bamboo to eat. They can spend around 14 hours per day eating bamboo.

Some pandas live in **nature reserves** in the city of Chengdu. Helpers look after young pandas and their parents. When the pandas have grown up, some are sent back to the wild.

This baby panda cub is only three months old.

CHINA'S RIVERS

The Yangtze River and the Yellow River are both well known in China. The Yangtze is the longest river in Asia. It is used to make **energy** for many Chinese people.

The Yangtze River

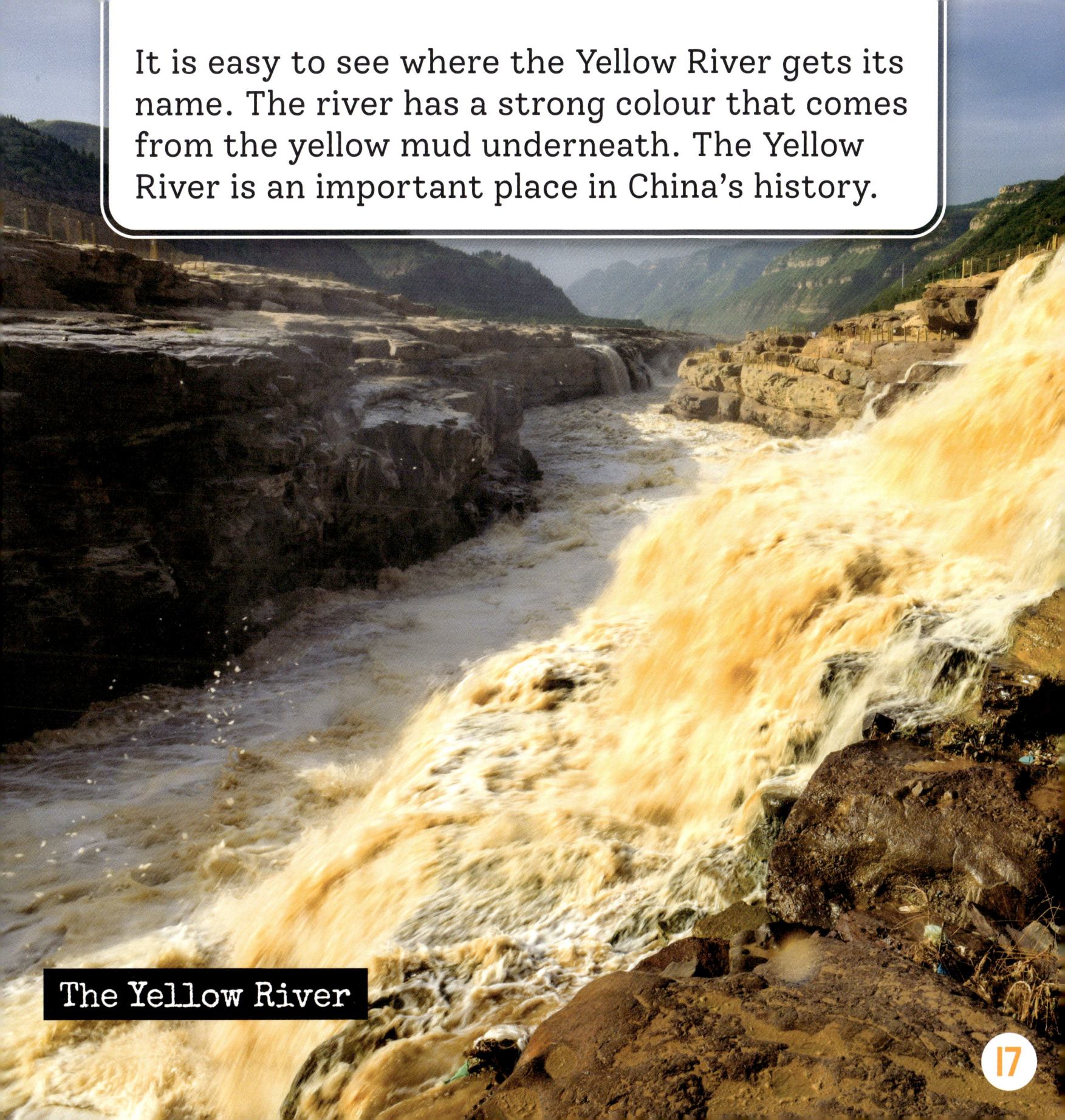

It is easy to see where the Yellow River gets its name. The river has a strong colour that comes from the yellow mud underneath. The Yellow River is an important place in China's history.

The Yellow River

TERRACOTTA ARMY

The Terracotta Army has clay <u>soldiers</u> and clay horses.

The city of Xi'an has one of China's biggest historical **discoveries**. Thousands of clay statues dressed like soldiers were found under ground in 1974. The statues are called the Terracotta Army.

Each statue is the size of a real person and has a different face. The statues were made for China's first **emperor**, who wanted to have guards with him even after he died.

China's first emperor was called Qin Shi Huangdi.

AMAZING BUILDINGS

The Forbidden City

The Forbidden City in Beijing is also important in Chinese history. Many of China's emperors lived here with their families. The Forbidden City has thousands of rooms, which are covered in Chinese dragon decorations.

The Hanging Monastery is much smaller than the Forbidden City, but it is still impressive. The building hangs from the side of a mountain. The **monastery** was used by people from three different Chinese religions.

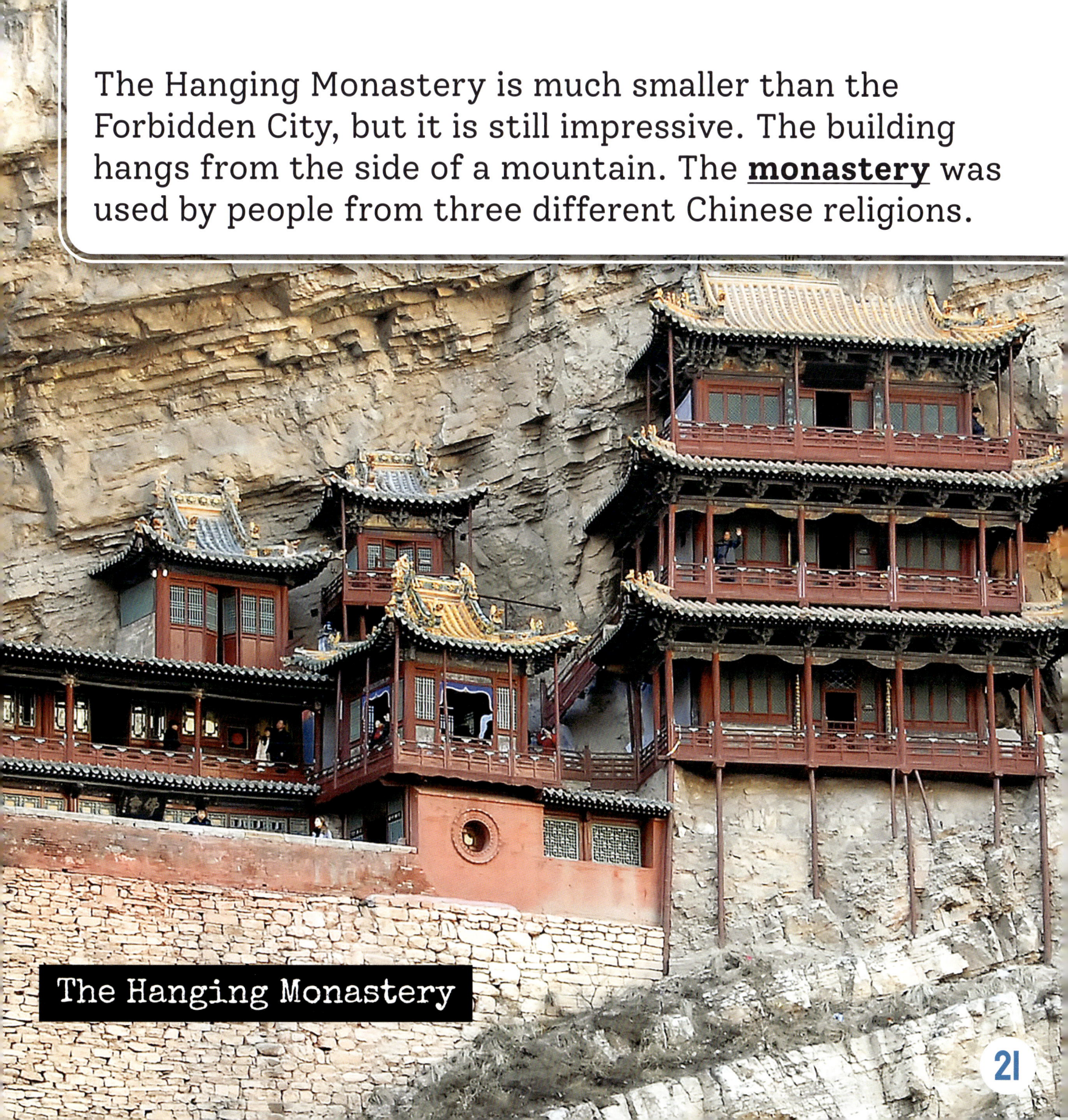

The Hanging Monastery

BEFORE YOU GO...

The Great Wall of China

Make sure to see the Great Wall of China if you get the chance. The wall was built by many emperors over thousands of years. The wall is over 20,000 kilometres long!

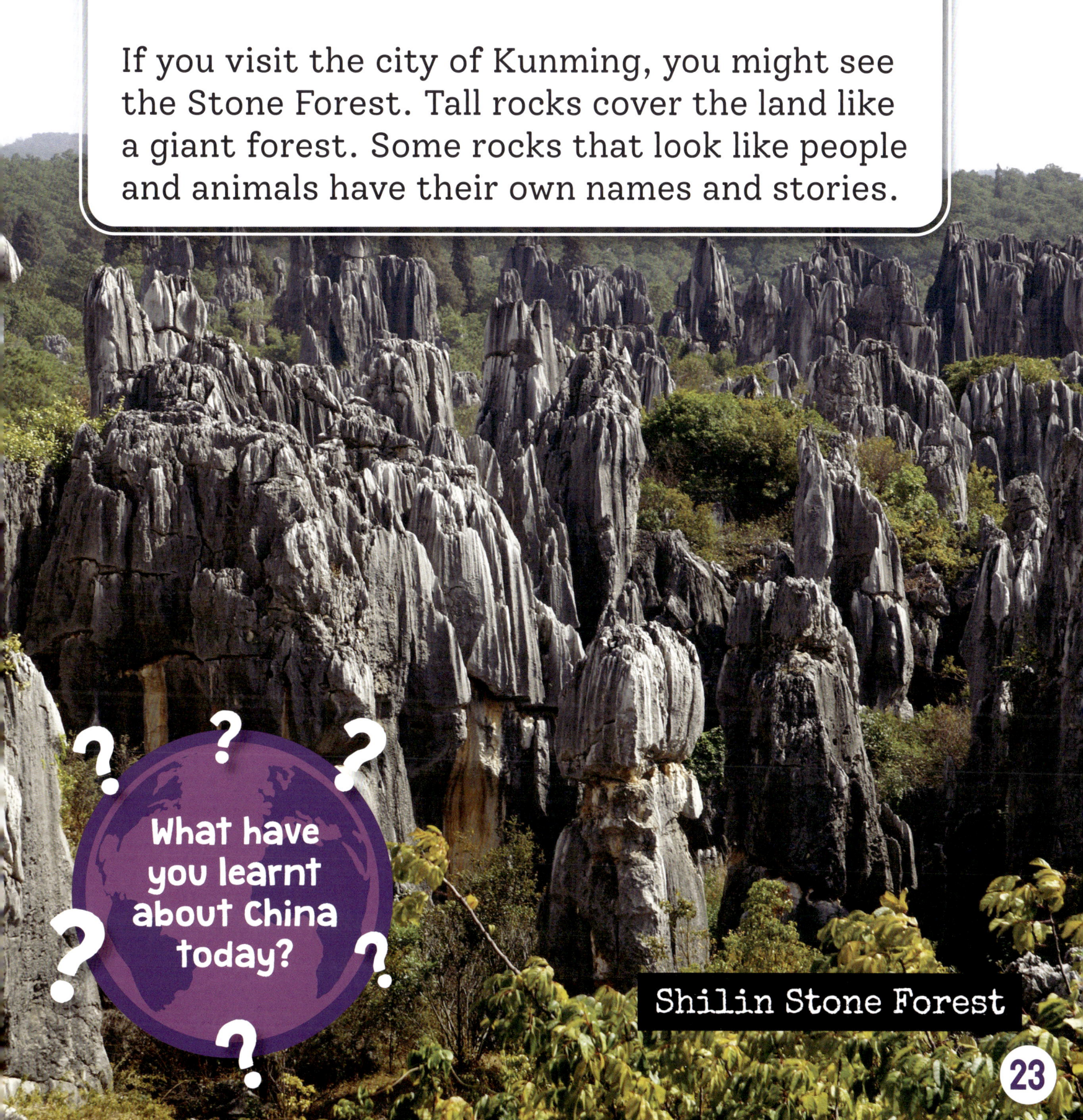

If you visit the city of Kunming, you might see the Stone Forest. Tall rocks cover the land like a giant forest. Some rocks that look like people and animals have their own names and stories.

What have you learnt about China today?

Shilin Stone Forest

GLOSSARY

borders	lines that show where one place ends and another begins
celebration	a special event that people come together to enjoy
discoveries	places or things that have been found for the first time
emperor	the ruler of a large area of land called an empire
energy	a type of power, such as light or heat, that can be used to do something
modern	something that is new and different from the past
monastery	a religious building that is home to monks or nuns
nature reserves	areas of land meant for keeping plants and animals protected in their normal environment
soldiers	people who fight as a group, usually for a leader

INDEX

buildings 8–9, 21

celebrations 10–11

dragons 10, 20

emperors 19–20, 22

forests 14, 23

history 9, 17, 20

mountains 14, 21

rice 11–12

statues 18–19